CU00900702

PUT TITLE HERE

~ An anthology of poems ~

By Jacob Shelley

Margaret,

I hope you enjoy the
book!

Happy Reading,

First published January 2015

Printed by Create Space

Cover art by Melissa Holden

Copyright© Jacob Shelley 2015

The moral right of the author has been asserted.

All rights reserved. No part of this publication may be reproduced,
stored in a retrieval system, or transmitted in any form by any
means without the written permission of the author, nor be
circulated in any form of binding or cover other than that in which
it is published and without a similar condition being imposed upon
the subsequent purchaser.

ISBN-13: 978-1507805695

ISBN-10: 1507805691

For my Mum and Dad – the greatest and most

inspirational people I have ever known

CONTENTS

Food, Food, Food!

Puzzle Box

This is England

Home

Yellow

The Last Deserters

Parents

November 5th

Amazon

Before Today

Today

After Today (Tomorrow)

The Beat of the Drum

A Life of Rhyme

Dreams vs Nightmares

My World

Christmas Tree

Good Old Santa Clause

New Year

Trench Song

Astronaut

The Gears of Time

A River of Tears

The Stranger I Thought I Knew

The War Known as Great

A Killer Concoction

Dragon

Alone

Mother

Father

All Day

The Point of Love

Olympic Spirit

The Archers Bow

Ping Pong Paddling

The Fire of Sportsmanship

The Many Flags

Five rings

Gymnastic Fantastic

Waterways

Olympiad Origins

Torch Bearer

Summer Fun

Oceans

Changing Tides

School Time

Sun, Sea, You and Me

The Ticking Clock

Gods and Monsters

Beyond the Woods

Does Cupid Know?

The Armistice

The Beginning is the End

Money's Kiss

Devils Roots

Playing with Heartstrings

Bubbles

From Dawn to Dusk

The Prize Giving

One More Story

The Coming and Going of Christmas

Techno Trap

Alien (Where is everyone?)

Put Title Here

The Blitz

A Poet's Destiny

The Stone Eye

We Are the Dead

Clock

Crowd

Have Your Say

By the Light of the Moon

Brimstone Inferno

The Human Condition

My Identity

Black Hole

Superhero

The Blank Page

Forever Young (co-written with Elysia Salmon)

Army in Red (co-written with Elysia Salmon)

Siren Song

H_2O

Animal Collection

The Earthworm

The Wire Man

The Gingerbread Man

A Philosophy on Fun

Blood Rose

INTRODUCTION

This anthology has no particular structure, but rather jumps from
one theme to another, much the way that the mind jumps from one
thought to the next. The collection acts as a train of thought,
following from one poem to the next, rather than boxing them up
into categories. It flows organically, following my journey over the
past four years, and the poems have been organised into the
original order in which they were written to reflect this. It's a
mental repository for whatever ideas came into my head and
inspired me to write, be it war, love, suffering or something
random like the number 8.

Many things have inspired me to write over the years, in particular
the historic events of World War One and my experiences of life,
love, family and the world around me. Inspiration often comes
from the most unlikely of places, but I have learned that the
greatest inspiration will come from those around you.

*"Creativity is a great motivator because it makes people interested
in what they are doing. Creativity gives hope that there can be a
worthwhile idea. Creativity gives the possibility of some sort of
achievement to everyone. Creativity makes life more fun and more
interesting" – Edward de Bono*

So without further ado…

Asian Lion

Roar! I scare away the birds,

I jump upon my prey,

Down falls another wild pig,

Another well spent day.

I drag the carcass to the den,

My cubs they mew with joy,

We all devour chunks of meat when

Suddenly I heard a noise.

Footsteps, going through the grass,

Coming right this way,

Then I see their heads poke out,

Humans! Not today!

I roar and gather up my cubs,

We scatter out of sight,

We stop by the riverbank, my cubs shivering in fright.

Then the footsteps come again,

Louder, closer still,

An arrow flies out of the bush and straight towards my head,

I duck, the arrow flies right past, and hits a tree instead.

I tell my cubs to scatter, I'll fight them on my own,

I give out a tremendous roar, and out the Humans come.

I run across the grassland,

The Humans close behind,

Quickly I must war the pride,

We're running out of time.

Whoosh! An arrow hits my side,

I tumble to the ground,

Whoosh! Another arrow hits,

I do not make a sound.

The world around me blackens,

We were the hunters once,

But now we are the hunted.

As the world grows ever darker still,

I give one final roar,

Then I hope the pride escaped,

And close my eyes once more.

We lions are endangered,

Unlike the common cat,

Soon we will all be extinct,

And that my friend, is that.

The Plague

It's all so far away now,

The plague that took my peaceful home,

The awful airborne spread disease.

I see them in my darkest nightmares,

Dying right in front of me,

Screaming in the night.

The creaking carts upon the cold, cobbled streets,

Hauling away the dead,

The bloody sign of Christ upon the rotting wooden doors.

The putrid pungent smell of death and damp decay,

The rats within the stinking slimy sewers,

Carrying the abomination.

It spreads across the whole wide world,

Extinguishing all in sight,

It has no mercy.

Plague doctors come to poke and prod the dead,

And take away the suffering,

The plague will kill us all.

Bodies buried in the exact same grave,

Hundreds upon hundreds of haunting rows,

This thing is but a cold hearted killer.

The horrors of this beast,

This creature, the Devil's advocate.

We've died and gone to hell.

Love's Last Lady

My heart breaks over her,

I could not open my mouth,

Behind the dark veil

I wished myself to hate.

Love's days did bite

Curses on the body

The wedding cake, but not the honeymoon.

A wardrobe of pebbles,

Then stabbed with red,

And puce,

My body bursting in its slow slewed corpse.

Day did remember the sweetheart,

Who lost me in green hands,

And awake, in some dead nights,

Yellowing in the mirror.

The Wonder of Winter

Snowflakes falling on the ground,

Snowballs flying round and round,

Looking at the leafless trees,

Flowers drooping on their knees,

Ice has frozen on the ground,

Winter's quiet, not a sound,

Snowman, snowman in my sight,

More snow's fallen in the night,

Woolly hats and gloves and scarves,

Throwing snowballs makes us laugh,

Coat's and boots and wellies too,

Got out my snow fort! Shoo! Shoo! Shoo!

Skiing, sledging that's for me,

And a cup of Cocoa with my tea.

The Call of Nature

The wasp, the trout, the drunken bee,

Sitting at the heart of an aged tree,

The mouse and the nest,

With wheat grown old,

The thunder and lightning,

Sound so bold,

The wind of the rainbow,

The shell of the nut,

The corn but the tulip,

Timid but proud.

Sleep and the wind,

Dreamless and breaking,

The falling of dew,

On hills of ice,

Which polar bears roam,

The stones of the desert,

Which no creature owns.

Sleep and the wind,

Dreamless but breaking

This is the poem

Of all nature's making.

Unforgotten Memories

A ribboned coat,

A season's red,

The smoke of honour,

In England's name,

The mark of a schoolboy,

A torch in the flame,

The breathless hush,

That followed his fame.

A river of rallies,

The death of the host,

The captain's final word,

Year by year is set,

How could he dare forget

The night that death had brimmed it's banks?

The colonel dead and blackening pitch,

The regiment with the lost of mind,

He knew he had to leave behind,

The blinding light, and killing shame,

Roll up to play, and name the game.

Leaving Home

A ham jar full of wild flowers,

A dog and candle bearer,

The lunch packed in the basket of her bicycle,

Not knowing how to say goodbye.

She hesitated,

Then left without a word,

And rode towards the church,

Leaving who had cared for her these long years behind.

She cleared wild parsley,

And pulled up a few nettles,

And rode into the sunlight,

Inbetween the wild flowers,

Growing down the lane.

As her grandfather read her note,

He locked her bedroom door,

And picked the last of the wild flowers,

Growing down the lane.

The Great Monsoon

An eternity of marble dust,

The moon's translucent gold,

Sands soft naming,

As the days grow old,

The reign of sun is waning,

Time waves the water underfoot,

And falling from the air,

Dandelion sunlight and clouded treachery,

Points from a clock hand,

To the darkening sky.

One, two, the river burst its banks,

Flowing across the fields,

Reaching towards the full moon.

As always, at this time of year,

There is the great monsoon.

London is No Place for Me

I sit upon this squalid rock,

As I stare out to sea,

I squint, and through the misty fog,

Ten boats are passing me.

Some are heading out to war,

Some to faraway lands,

But then I see a sailing boat,

That can help me with my plans,

I want to get away from here,

This place will be my grave,

As in the fog of industrial London,

No one thinks to save,

A little boy that roams the streets,

That escaped from his workhouse home,

And wants to see the whole wide world,

And never be alone.

I sit upon this squalid rock,

As I stare out to sea,

I squint, and through the misty fog,

Ten boats are passing me.

Waiting for the Bell

We go inside,
 And unpack out things.
We're waiting for the bell.

The teacher gets up,
'Open your textbooks please'
We're waiting for the bell.

We copy from the board,
And someone falls asleep.
We're waiting for the bell.

I get on with my project,
And organise my coursework.
I'm waiting for the bell.

Then we're told to pack away,
And hear that joyful sound.
We listen to the bell.
School is over, and we are free!

The Sinful Form of Man

The unforsaken darkness,

Aggrieved over death and decay,

The families come weeping

To the graveyard that very day.

A sanctuary of madness,

The decrepit forms of mind,

Manacles of hate and fear

Enchain the man behind.

Just like a malignant growth,

The vengeance spreads and drains,

Every essence of humanity

Making you a void.

The mind just breaks and shatters,

It I as fragile as a vase,

Whilst death is the quickest way

The marks shall never fade from the lives we touch.

Trust

Trust shall always be there,
In everybody's lives,
It can sometimes be the only thing,
To set the truth apart from lies.

It tells you who your friends are,
Be careful who you trust,
Your enemies will lure you in,
So resist them all you must.

Trust can bring some good things,
But brings some bat things too,
Either way the trust can go,
Which way is up to you.

Trust is like a mirror,
You can repair it when it breaks.
But you will ALWAYS see
Cracks in your reflection.

Brother

You always have been there for me,

Even when I'm blue,

And on your very special day,

I'll do the same for you,

I remember when I held you,

As a tiny baby boy,

I remember how you looked at me,

With a smile full of joy,

Even though you're growing up,

I'll always love you still,

Because our bond is like superglue,

And my brother, you will always be.

So nave a very special day,

And keep this in your heart,

As from one bother to another,

You make me the proudest of them all.

The Poppy Field

A sea of blood red petals,

Rustling in the breeze,

The unforgotten message, that

the poppies tell to us.

A symbol of the peace we have,

And those who fought and died for us,

The poppy field stays standing,

Swaying in the breeze.

Read By Candlelight

Sitting on the candlelit desk,

The letter in his hands,

He reads his words carefully.

Finding out the envelope,

He slips it all inside,

And seals it with the wax.

The mailman came to take the letter,

And spirited it away,

As only can it be read by candlelight.

How?

How do people change?

Why do people change?

How are things made?

How do things work?

How do I do this?

How shall I say it?

How is that possible?

How is this right?

How is life a mystery?

How come nobody is answering my questions?

8

This poem has eight syllables,

Eight syllables on every line,

You can count them if you want to,

But telling you just saves more time.

Eight syllables on every line.

The Autumn Leaves

The crisp red,

The yellowish brown,

The autumn leaves

fall on the ground.

They twist and turn,

In the coldish breeze,

And form tornadoes

Around your knees.

The autumn leaves,

Migrate from the tree,

Leaving bare branches

for all to see.

The once crisp red,

The mouldish brown,

Those autumn leaves

are now part of the ground.

That Monster Under My Bed

That monster under my bed,

Is always on the lookout,

For my swinging ankles over the edge,

So he can pull me under.

I see his eyes in the mirror,

And his claws when I rummage

for that box of stuff from years ago,

Those things that time forgot.

He thinks he is real scary,

And an oh so mighty beast.

But the thing is,

I'm older now, and that monster,

Oh, that once terrifying monster

doesn't scare me one bit.

Nope.

Not ever.

Instead, he hides and cowers in fear,

Of the man above the bed.

Boys

Two boys,

Make more noise,

Than anything I know,

When they're quiet,

Not causing a riot,

Saying little at all.

But we presser the noise,

Riots shouts and all,

'Cause boys will be boys.

<u>Stars</u>

The stars in the sky do twinkle,

When I look up and dream,

And imagine what secrets they hold,

I wish that one day I could be

amongst them,

But 'till then, I shall gaze up at the stars.

Waiting

You have no idea what it's like,

Waiting.

Waiting for something to arrive,

Waiting for something to happen,

Just waiting.

The boredom eats at my insides

as I sit here and simply wait.

I don't know what I'm waiting for,

I don't know why I'm waiting,

All I know is that I'm waiting,

Just waiting,

Sitting here waiting.

Do you even understand a word I'm saying?

The Hourglass

The golden sand held within

a turning glass pendulum,

Counting down the time until

each grain of sand has passed

through the funnel from top to bottom.

It stands there elegantly,

Counting each and every grain of sand that passes,

Whittling away the time, until,

It turns again,

Never stopping,

Always moving,

The hourglass keeps turning,

Counting down to zero,

As it stands upon the mantelpiece.

A Typical Teenage Life

They rise in the dawn while I stay asleep,

And they prepare for their long and hard day,

I don't get up until I'm shouted at,

Called lazy and told to go to school,

My mum labours away at home all day,

And my dad 'works' to earn the money,

While I go to school and 'learn' some stuff.

They must work because they are old,

And I,

Must receive an education in what?

Some say I'm lazy, but so what?

Who cares?

I'm living the typical teenage life.

The Sweetshop

Every day I pass the sweetshop window,

And every day I peek and look inside,

My heart pounds fast, for what I see,

Would make any child giddy with glee;

Rows upon rows upon rows of jars,

Filled with every sweet,

Stacks upon stacks upon stacks of choc bars,

Oh! What a sumptuous treat!

And there,

Behind the receiving desk,

Lies the keeper,

The Kandy man,

A guardian with such power that

he governs all the lands;

Of sherbert sweets and marshmallow clouds,

Rustling in the breeze,

To lollipop lampposts and candyfloss trees

that will bring you to your knees.

I'm dribbling again. I must stop that.

Where was I? Oh, yes…

The world of the most amazing things,

And to enter is such a small fare,

Such so that children will do anything,

To get inside of there.

I draw my eyes from the window,

That place, my childhood love,

Now a baron boarded place,

It left me with the passing winds,

And died without a trace.

The bus is heading down the road,

Away from candy cone lane,

To lose the entrance to paradise,

I consider quite a shame.

The Darkness

They are a darkness to the light,

A hatred to your love,

They are everything you will never be,

And they are the things you see in your darkest nightmares,

They are the shadow in the corner of your eye,

And the ting that walks behind you.

They are the creak of a board in an empty room,

And the voices of the invisible.

Everyone has irrational fears,

But I know something.

They're not irrational,

They're real.

The Easter Island Heads

If ever I have seen a group of

statues standing high,

Watching very vacantly

as time passes them by,

Expressions that are cold as stone,

With an ever distant gaze,

They've been there since the dawn of time,

And will remain till the end of days.

Their face the size of twenty men,

The giants of their land,

Way out there on Easter Island,

Where forever they shall stand.

<u>Silence</u>

Silence is real,

Silence is all around you,

Silence is always with you,

Silence is in you,

Silence is all we'll be,

And silence is all we need.

The Roots of the Library

The forest stands so vast and tall,

To which every eye can see,

But deep, deep down below it all,

Hidden from you and me,

The forest, born from rows of books

but way down underneath,

The instincts of another life,

Do surface from their sheath.

For every night, on the stroke of twelve,

The library comes alive,

Roots are spread; trees stand true,

Desperate to survive.

The sunlight comes with unknown agony,

As the trees reform to books,

The library is more deadly than

It ever, ever looks.

The Corridor

The hallowed halls,

With wooden floors,

The flaky paint,

And creaky doors,

The dim lit rooms,

And dusty books,

The grey stained windows,

With ancient looks,

The corridor at the end of the line,

That's been empty and untouched since the beginning of time.

The End

The beginning and the end are all the same,

Just different squares on the life board game,

To get to the end I must succeed,

At everything life throws at me,

From square to square I progress through life,

Through marriage, parenthood and retired strife,

And once I'm back round to the only square one,

I can leave this world happy,

Knowing I've lived and I'm done.

The Blue Tits

The blue tits do cheep,

In their bird box nest,

As the mother comes home to feed,

And they poke out their heads,

And stare all around,

Eating caterpillars with greed.

The blue tits do jump,

When they land on the ground,

Desperately trying to fly,

While other than that,

Avoiding the cat,

That most definitely is sly.

The blue tits do soar,

Around in the sky,

As the look for a mate to breed,

And from my point of view,

I think that they do,

Look very splendid indeed.

Pet

I long to return to the endless blue sky,

Where I swooped and soared with glee,

I dived through the clouds, and flew up so high,

Oh, how I long to be free.

I long to return to the fruit bearing tree,

Where are dawn chorus used to begin,

And where we would eat berries until we could burst,

Oh, how I long to be free.

Then the humans came.

I long to return to the birds that I know,

With the nest, my family and me,

Through the tears that now flow, I will always know,

That a prisoner, or 'pet' I shall be.

Gone but not forgotten

In loving memory of my Great Granddad. You are dearly missed x

They say you only realise what you have when it has gone,

Let me tell you that's exactly what it's like,

They say that you must be strong, and that you must move on,

But sometimes, it's just too hard, and doesn't feel right.

Losing someone close to you is the hardest thing to feel,

And also the hardest thing to understand,

But you know that there are memories that you never will forget,

Like the first time that you held their loving hand.

So hold them dearly in your hearts,

And in your memories,

And with you all our thoughts will always be,

As even though you're gone, and we have to move on,

Nothing can be done to fill your gap.

For we love you and we miss you,

But you're always in our hearts,

And in anything but the honest truth,

You never will depart.

As you are gone but not forgotten,

You shall never be forgotten,

Until the end and all thereafter,

Forever, your memories shall stand.

The Life of Art

The life of art is true obscure,

It can go through any door,

Artists take on many styles,

That take up time and long lost whiles,

Artists come and artists go,

But art itself won't leave, oh no,

Art is an eternal thing,

A pictures way of trying to sing.

The Beginning

At first, there was nothing,

No time, no space, no life.

Then, some say what happened next,

Is that a bang ignited all of reality,

Forming dust and rocks and gas,

Swirling around to form stars and galaxies.

Like a snow shaker in your hands.

But that was 14 billion years ago,

And the universe has progressed,

Forming solar systems, black holes and nebulae,

Should I mention all the rest?

Constantly expanding,

Constantly creating,

Constantly amazing.

We owe this to the beginning.

The Gift

The weirdest gift I ever got?

A star.

Somewhere out there in the darkened sky,

Lies the star that was given to me,

Every night I search the stars,

And hope it is one I will see.

So far, I haven't found it yet,

But one day soon I will,

I'll fly to it if necessary,

And even further still,

Space can be so mighty big,

But if it weren't at all,

Where would you put the stars?

That gift of mine is still out there,

Still turning,

Waiting to be received.

Snapshot

Click!

The image is a sudden blur,

The focus out of range,

The features of the image fade,

The settings need to be changed.

Click!

This time, people can be seen,

Their features clear as day,

The background is slightly out of focus,

In a very clever way.

Click!

This time the picture is just right,

The confetti, church and car,

Everyone is smiling,

And you're the happiest by far,

In the snapshot of your wedding.

The Last Spartan

I wander through the cloudy dust,

My armour is spattered with blood,

As the mist clears, what I gaze upon,

Makes me drop my shield with a thud.

Fire, licking the edge of the sky,

And spreading horizon wide,

As I watch my city, my home, my love,

my fortune, faith and pride,

Sparta, burning to the ground.

The Persians marching forwards,

Taking revenge on the Spartan paradise,

My heart begins to pound,

My comrades lay upon the floor,

Along with my Persian foes,

I must move on and continue my quest,

Although my heart is filled with woes.

I wear the clothes of an ancient race,

And I march on the desolate land,

Even though I still live on,

All else turns to sand.

For I, am the last Spartan.

Time Machine

If I possessed a time machine,

There are endless places I would go,

Medieval times, the future perhaps,

Or maybe the first ever theatre show.

If I possessed a time machine,

There would be lots of sights to see,

Like the fall of troy, and putting man on the moon,

Or the first British monarchy.

If I possessed a time machine,

There's loads that I would do,

The Egyptians, Aztecs, Incas and Mayans,

Perhaps an alien zoo.

If I possessed a time machine,

I have endless lists of things to say,

But I think that I'll stay here tonight,

And use it on another day.

Life Sonnet

From birth to death I shall enjoy it all,

The rising and thee falling of the sun,

Through thick and thin until the day I fall,

I will only lay down when I have won,

Wherever I shall go I always will,

Never forget the things that I have done,

I will do anything to keep time still,

So I can view life with no need to run,

I will remember and never regret,

The path I've taken to this paradise,

I think that I would never dare forget,

That when things die life becomes cold as ice,

It's always worth the trouble and the strife,

So listen to this sonnet about life.

The Lost Kingdom

The kingdom from so long ago,

The one we never found,

So long ago it did exist,

We believe it's underground.

With buildings tall and cities vast,

This kingdom ruled the plains,

It even had technology,

Like boats and cars and trains.

With quantities of jewels and gold,

Beyond our human dreams,

It makes us truly wonder how

the city broke down at the seams.

The kingdom of a thousand kings,

The refuge for first men,

By now this once magnificent place,

Is probably a pile of sand.

The kingdom from so long ago,

The one we never found,

So long ago it did exist,

It's deep, deep underground.

Food, Food, Food!

Oh, food!

Glorious food!

There is so much that I can say,

There's thousands beginning with each letter,

What should I eat today?

A is for apples in sweet apple pie,

B is for banoffee sauce,

C, c, what could it be?

Cis for curry, of course!

D is for doughnuts with jelly and sprinkles,

E is for eggs of all form,

F is for fries, the best of the lot,

Just make sure that your food is all warm.

G is for grapes that are made into wine,

H is for hamburger cheese,

I is for ice cream, flavours so sweet,

It brings me to my knees.

J is for jelly, all bouncy and hyper,

K is a mystery meal,

L is for lemons, all sour and squishy,

But I'm sure we can strike up a deal.

M is for meringue, all sweet and all tasty,

N is for noodles of course,

O is for oatmeal, which everyone knows,

Is a favourite food for the horse.

P is for pizza, the Italian kind,

Q is for queues to get in,

R is for ravioli, which if no cooked right,

Will simply end up in the bin.

S is for sweets, the best of all friends,

T is for T-bone steak,

U is for the ultimate lunch,

But you might just need a break.

V is for veal, which nobody likes,

W is for Worcestershire sauce,

X is for nothing that springs to my mind,

Which is a shame, as I want my next course.

Y is for yoghurt, lumpy or not,

Z oh, Z what to do,

For there is no food I can think of,

That will EVER rhyme with you.

Oh, food!

Glorious food!

There is not much more that I can say,

If I eat any more I might explode,

O I think I'll return on another day.

Puzzle Box

To escape I get a puzzle box,

And I must get inside,

If I want to survive in here,

I must get out, not hide,

This puzzle tests my very mind,

Until the answer I do find,

I've solved the puzzle to set me free,

And my reward is the prison key.

This is England (World War One monologue)

As the clouds of evil descend once more,

We must be vigilant,

Every man, woman and child must stand tall,

And do their duty.

For those we have been forced to place our trust in,

Have failed us.

We have been abandoned.

But do not lose hope,

As citizens of the country unite,

We can do this.

And tonight, I need you all with me,

For on this day, in this place,

We shall make our stand.

We will drive out the forces of darkness that threaten us,

And rightfully defend what is ours!

I cannot guarantee we will all return,

But if we never come back,

Never mourn us,

Never miss us,

Never forget us.

For today is the day we rise higher than ever before.

This is our last stand, and we will keep fighting,

No matter what the cost.

For we are English,

And this. Is. England!

Home

Home is where the heart is,

Of course that saying is true,

Maternal instinct for home are always there,

Every second of your life.

Yellow

Yellow is the slab of cheese that sits upon your plate,

Yellow is bananas peeled, the ones the monkey ate,

Yellow is our scorching sun that sizzles all year round,

Yellow is the new-born chicks and their joyful chirping sound,

Yellow is the buttercups, as graceful as can be,

Yellow can mean danger, like the signs you may see,

Yellow is the plastic face of a Lego figures head,

Yellow is the colour of grass when it finally is dead,

Yellow are the pages of an ever ancient book,

Yellow with a shine or tint gives gold a special look,

Yellow is a smiling face that can easily be found,

And yellow is a colour that is welcome all year round.

The Last Deserters

I

He was a great man,

And a hero to many,

But it had to end.

II

Close friends only knew,

The troubles that lay ahead,

And why he left them.

III

The war was over,

And still he did not return,

A hope that failed them.

IV

He had let them down,

The man who vowed to save them,

And hid in the night.

V

Now he can't return,

To the place where he began,

To redeem himself.

VI

He was a lost cause,

Following the winds of change,

And was gone by noon.

VII

Life did hold no joy,

For he who deserted them,

Now lays in the dust.

VIII

The ground beneath us,

Is his and the others graves,

The last deserters.

Parents

When I was young the parents were

the force to fight against,

Then they were to comfort you,

A shield, a solid fence.

Now I see that's all quite real,

They'll always love you still,

MOST things that they say are true,

And they are always looking out for you.

November 5th

The pile of wood and disused things,

That will easily catch on fire,

Throw on some oil above and below,

To make the flames go higher.

Throw in the torch and watch things explode,

As the bonfire rears into life,

Cutting through air and the dark of the night,

Like butter cut by a hot knife.

The people arrive and festivities start,

With sparklers and glow sticks galore,

The roasting of marshmallows on a spiked wooden stick,

The taste leaves you wanting more.

Now it is time for the display to begin,

And with a flash the fireworks are sent flying,

The sound and the colour mesmerising all in range,

Everyone staring at the sky without sighing.

The bang and the boom and the sparkling flash,

As the children scream out in delight,

And when it's all over they head to the chippie,

Glad that they had a good night.

As the ashes grow dim and the sun starts to rise,

The remains of a guy is still there,

And the lesson or motto of this celebration,

Is one that is easily shared.

"Remember, remember the 5th of November,

Gunpowder, treason and plot."

Forget we must not.

Amazon

As I stand within this feat of nature,

I feel compelled.

I want to dive under the silvery skin

of this ever moving snake,

And swim through the heart of the commotion.

I can feel the small pebbles under my feet.

I want to feel the silence,

And hear the sense of being underwater,

Without a need to breathe.

The reeds along the bank act as a marker,

For the territory of those

who live upon the back of this giant,

Compared to them I feel like an intruder,

Easily removed or worse.

With an uneasy sense of insignificance,

I wade over to the bank where

my shorts and backpack lay.

As the fish swim around my feet,

In the crystal clear body of this deity,

I watch my friends play on,

Along the back of the Amazon snake.

Before Today

Before today we were the losing side,

And we did lose everything but our faith,

Before today we had very little pride,

In the safety and survival of our race,

Before today we were the slaves and poor,

But soon that all shall be turned around,

Before today we lived upon the floor,

But now we push our enemies to the ground.

Today

Today we make our stand and put up a fight,

We will prove our faith in what we believe,

Today, the leader, our guide, is on our side,

As we vacate the space they made for us beneath,

Today we form a group that cannot fall,

And will show our foes that we are truly good,

Today we shall revel in it all,

For evil, here we come, you knew we would.

After Today (Tomorrow)

After today we will be the reigning champs,

Our enemies will take our lowly place,

After today we will have luxuries,

Swap our rags for cotton, wool and lace,

After today we rise, never to fall,

And shall have riches beyond our wildest dreams,

After today we shall have it all,

Until our species breaks down at the seams.

Tomorrow, we will be dust.

The Beat of the Drum

Dum, Dum, Dum, Dum,

We march to the beat of the drum,

Dum, Dum, Dum, Dum,

Together we march as one,

Dum, Dum, Dum, Dum,

In uniform we stride,

Dum, Dum, Dum, Dum,

Carrying our nations pride,

Dum, Dum, Dum, Dum,

One by one we fall,

Dum, Dum, Dum, Dum,

Until few are left if at all,

Dum, Dum, Dum, Dum,

I march to the beat of the drum,

Dum, Dum, Dum, Dum,

I am the last surviving son.

A Life of Rhyme

Now that I have found a way,

With freedom of expression,

I can convey to you my every thought,

Once I have your full attention.

Through poetry I show you all,

My thoughts and feelings aloud,

Whether they be happy, embarrassed, angry, sad,

confused, depressed or proud,

This is my way of speaking out,

And defining who I am,

For the time has come for me to grow,

Into a lion from a lamb.

I am entirely what you see,

I am guilty of no crime,

But to achieve my best and speak my soul,

I live a life of rhyme.

Dreams vs Nightmares

There are things that you can never quite remember,

But what you always wish would just come true,

The blissful times that never really happened,

And every one is unique in some way too.

But sometimes dreams get out of hand,

And the nightmare comes along,

It torments you inside you head,

And can stay there all night long,

As it sings its darkened song.

Dreams can be a dangerous thing,

As anyone can see,

But also, sometimes, now and then,

They can set some people free.

My World

I go there when I close my eyes,

It's a place to be alone,

No one else can get in unless I,

Give them a key.

Here, I am secure.

Unlike in what we call 'reality',

Here I am safe.

Nothing can ever hurt me,

In my world,

I can indulge in whatever I can imagine,

Without fear, danger or sadness,

Without rules or control. I am the king.

For my world is a fortress,

It is all but impenetrable,

It is here that I am myself,

And I can live happily ever after.

In my world.

Christmas Tree

It is such a sight of majestic beauty,

In the corner of our living space,

It sums up this time in two single words,

And puts a smile on everyone's face,

Decorated in any way that we please,

The layout will change every year,

Presents placed under it for everyone,

Bringing some joy and some cheer!

With lighting and tinsel and big bulbous baubles,

It gleams in the light of the fire,

A big star on top, chocolate treats hidden all over,

It makes the room look so much brighter!

Whenever we have somebody stop by,

It's the very first thing that they see,

Their responses of wow! Would you just look at that?

It's a wonderful Christmas tree.

Good Old Santa Clause

A jolly red outfit with white fluffy edges,

And a belt that nearly won't fit,

A big fluffy beard and a red and white hat,

That was Santa when I was a kid!

He'd pop down your chimney and leave you some gifts,

Piled all neatly under your tree,

He'd eat all the cookies I had left out that night,

And down the glass of whiskey!

He'd write me a note saying 'ta very much'

And back up the chimney he goes,

Once he got stuck, a real bit of luck,

And he sneezed from the soot in his nose!

Then he flies off my rooftop in a sleigh pulled by reindeer,

And just as he flew out of sight,

He turned, saw my face, smiled and called

'Merry Christmas to all, and to all a good night!'

New Year

10

We're all anticipating,

9

What next year will bring,

8

Some hold parties and celebrations,

7

And people eat dance and sing,

6

A new year, a new leaf,

5

Everyone can start again,

4

For another the hundred and sixty five days,

3

But every now and then,

2

With happiness and joyful cheer,

1

The countdown is over, happy New Year!

Trench Song

We got bombed last night,

Got bombed the night before,

Probably bombed tonight,

But then we won't get bombed no more.

The trench is falling in,

There's craters all around,

No man's land is empty,

And there's not a bloody sound,

They keep on bombing us,

They keep on bombing us,

They keep on bombing us,

They keep on bombing us,

They keep on bombing us,

They keep on bombing us,

But after tonight we won't be bombed no more.

We were gassed last night,

Got gassed the night before,

Gonna get gassed tonight,

But then we won't get gassed no more.

The gas masks are no good,

The stench will still get through,

You have to hold your breath,

Or else the mustard will kill you.

They keep on gassing us,

They keep on gassing us,

They keep on gassing us,

They keep on gassing us,

They keep on gassing us,

They keep on gassing us,

But after tonight we won't be gassed no more.

Did a raid last night,

A raid the night before,

Another raid tonight,

But then I will not raid no more.

The men hang on the wire,

There's nothing they can do,

But be shot at by the Boche,

Until their skin turns black and blue.

We keep in raiding 'em,

We keep in raiding 'em,

We keep in raiding 'em,

We keep in raiding 'em,

We keep in raiding 'em,

We keep in raiding 'em,

But after tonight won't do a raid no more.

Sent over the top the other day,

Over the top the day before,

Going over the top tonight,

But won't go over the top no more.

It's a suicidal game,

And we don't want to die,

The judge will give us all court martial,

He don't need a reason why.

They send us over the top,

They send us over the top,

They send us over the top,

They send us over the top,

They send us over the top,

They send us over the top,

But after tonight I won't go over the top no more.

I survived last night,

Survived the night before,

I might survive tonight,

But then I won't survive no more.

My time is running out,

And the offensive's coming up,

And I have got the feeling,

That I just ran out of luck.

I might survive tonight,

I might survive tonight,

I might survive tonight,

I might survive tonight,

I might survive tonight,

I might survive tonight,

But after tonight I won't survive no more.

The home front doesn't know,

Don't know what's going on,

Down here at the front,

The think that nothing's going wrong.

Someone needs to state the facts,

And set the record straight,

Tell them all what's going on,

Before it's too late.

Tell them what's going on,

Tell them what's going on,

Tell them what's going on,

Tell them what's going on,

Tell them what's going on,

Tell them what's going on,

Tell them all what's going on before it's all too late.

Astronaut

An endless mass of space and stars,

Such experiences I long to have,

The endless view of the universe,

Revelling in its majesty,

Omnipotent and omniscient,

Nothing can compare,

Always the unanswerable,

Under a starlit heaven,

The endless skies do twinkle.

The Gears of Time

The endless gears of time,

That pull the both of us apart,

Force you to keep me locked away,

Within the confines of your heart,

The cogs that grind in motion,

Tear us both away,

To opposite ends of time and space,

And there we have to stay,

The countless time continuums,

That push me away from you,

The endless gears of time that strike the hour true,

For we can never be as one,

Our fates were never intertwined,

The gears of time have set their course,

And both of us were left behind.

The beats within my heart grow slow,

The cannot beat without you,

But the gears of time have locked away,

Our feelings from all to view.

A River of Tears

You've caused my heart to burst its banks,

My tears surround my view,

Of those who rose up through the ranks,

I should have feared the most from you.

You cut me down like it was

a sapling or a twig,

I shared my soul, my every thought,

And this is what you took.

The flood that does surround me now,

Is not of anger or of hate,

But more a question as of how,

Your being here was quite innate.

You stole my life,

You drained me dry,

And now this endless river of tears,

Is all that I can cry.

The Stranger I Thought I Knew

Suddenly you have become

a stranger in my life,

A person I entirely thought I knew,

We've been through so much together, trouble strife and all,

I never thought I'd drift away from you.

The era ends, we grow apart,

Our minds just change and grow,

Into another person that

we do not need to know.

You, are the stranger I thought I knew.

The War Known as Great

I

Our heroes rose and took the call,

They paid the sum of things to pay,

And out on Flanders fields they fall,

So we could be alive today.

II

We shall not forget the price

they paid, The final sacrifice

was made, by millions and felt as one,

By the passing of an English son.

III

Home at last, but not the same,

For war was not a joyous game,

Its horror shook him to his core,

And haunts his nights forever more.

IV

The bullets whiz across the sky,

Like a metal rain of rage,

The men were young, and died as such,

For wisdom only comes with age.

V

When war began, the men they sang,

With patriotic pride,

But as they fell, their final words…

'The politicians lied'

VI

As a VAD, what did I see,

But men who were torn to shreds,

For those who run in the face of the gun,

Have surely lost their heads.

VII

We won the war but lost the men,

The graves in France are stacked up high,

While veterans tell their tale of war,

The widowed women sit and cry.

A Killer Concoction

Eye of toad, and tail of newt,

Should surely cure the little brute,

Hair of cat, and blood of pig,

His bones will snap just like a twig,

Wing of bat, and dust of fairy,

This poison turns all nice things scary,

Mandrake root, and swampish ooze,

The little swine will surely lose,

Sting of nettle, and clover leaf,

The potion shall soon find its sheath,

And now for the most vital part,

A dragon's brain and witches wart,

One drop should surely be enough,

To stop the wicked monsters heart.

Dragon

Its scales gleam like crystal jewels,

Cast in the most entrancing light,

Its eyes are dark and black as coals,

Darker than the deepest depths of night,

Its wings spread wide across the field,

A shadow cast by evolutionary might,

Its legs are thick, and strong as trees,

To fill the villains hearts with fright,

It soars above our tiny world,

And drifts on currents like a kite,

Its fire from jaws so powerful, can

turn stone to crystal, and set all alight,

Its roar stops my enemies' hearts as they fall,

My dragon, is the best of all.

Alone

Be it by chance or a natural cause,

I will always be alone,

Controlled by an inhuman force,

I have always and never known,

It can drive the stables man insane,

Can drain your soul of joy and light,

Being alone is a permanent pain,

Like being lost in a forest in the dead of the night,

Alone I was, alone I am,

Alone I will always be,

I've lost my life, my mind, my soul,

For all eternity.

Mother

Matriarch of the household,

Omniscient and omnipotent,

There's nothing they can't do,

Here to look after you,

Every instinct primed,

Responses fast as lightning.

Father

Family man with kids at home,

Always hard at work,

The dedicated footie fan,

He loves his wife well and true,

Even his kids (when they don't annoy him),

Reaping the rewards of fatherhood.

All Day

You don't wake up until half past ten,

It's a horrible rainy day,

Who cares? You have nothing to do,

But stay in bed and play,

Your x-box, laptop, ps3, ds or I-pod too,

You could sleep again, or read a book,

The choice is up to you,

You just have to look,

You're ill or tired or just plain lazy,

But when anyone asks, you'll say,

Don't worry, I've got things to do,

So I'll stay in bed all day.

The Point of Love

It seems when courtly love prevails,

It hides within the knightly trees,

And lives to tell its mighty tales,

Of romance, passion and victories,

But also in that darkened wood,

A darker love, forbidden lies,

An obsessive, abominable love which should

never be seen by mortal eyes,

The other loves that take their shape,

Do twist and change as time goes by,

Like an endless, ever shifting drape,

Some loves, do well and truly die,

What is the point of human love

That fits the heart just like a glove?

Olympic Spirit

It's the wondrous event,

That is honourable to play,

On once every four years,

For just seventeen days,

It's the hours of training,

And the effort put in,

By the two hundred and five nations,

Trying to win,

The gold, the silver and the bronze,

The chance to stand up high,

And cheer upon the podium,

Some will even cry,

But the Olympic spirit isn't the win, or the victory,

It's the taking part that counts.

The Archers Bow

I close my eyes,

I focus my mind,

Everything else I leave behind,

I tighten my grip,

I pull on the string,

I must get this right if I want to win,

I release my shot,

It flies from the bow,

Will it hit the target? I hope so,

It hit's the board,

A perfect ten,

Now I have to do it again.

Ping Pong Paddling

Clack, clack, clack, clack,

The ball does fly from side to side,

Clack, clack, clack, clack,

In your hand the paddle flies,

Clack, clack, clack, clack,

Ping pong paddling all day long.

The Fire of Sportsmanship

The fire does burn,

Once every four years,

It draws out huge crowds,

And ruptures of cheers,

It signals the start,

Of the Olympic Games,

For hundreds of countries,

And thousands of names,

It signifies fairness,

Not cheating, just trying,

To be a good sportsman,

No faking or lying,

The fire of sportsmanship

Unites all athletes,

Under one blazing beacon of hope.

The Many Flags

They are the symbols,

Of each of the nations,

Their identity forged within,

The flags of old,

They go for gold,

All wanting to win.

The many flags,

That flap in the breeze,

Symbols of these,

Bonds of unity.

Five Rings

Five rings, five continents,

Brought together as one,

A symbol of hope, achievement and honour,

In an event that is sure to be fun,

Each colour can be found on any flag,

Flown throughout the world,

Union and sportsmanship,

The five rings represent,

A symbol every person knows,

And watches with intent,

Five rings that unify the world.

Gymnastic Fantastic

I dust my hands with powdered chalk,

To help me with my grip,

So when I grab the parallel bars,

They will not move or slip,

I balance myself with steady hands,

Upon the hanging rings,

I pull myself up with all my strength,

And do amazing things,

I spin around the pommel horse,

As I twist and twirl,

I show off all my fancy moves,

Like trying to impress a girl,

I bounce upon the trampoline,

I roll and twist and fall,

Of all he athletes in this place,

I might be best of all,

I stand atop the podium,

The gold hangs round my neck,

I am gymnastic fantastic!

Waterways

Butterfly, backstroke, and Front crawl,

We move along the waterways,

Using techniques that we know best,

And that we practice every day,

Breast stroke and doggy paddle too,

We're cheered by the fans

To win the gold and finish the race,

And do the best we can.

Olympiad Origins

In Greece the Olympiad story begins,

Many thousands of years in the past,

The games consisted of athletic men,

Competing and running fast,

The sports developed, changed and grew,

Then women joined the game,

The flag with five Olympic rings,

Gave it the household name,

From ancient Greece to the modern world,

The origins stand strong as stone.

Torch Bearer

I dress in the top of white and grey,

Embossed with golden text,

The number on my left shoulder is one,

I know what happens next,

I reach the street where I shall run,

The crowds packed on both sides,

The officials turn up, I'm handed the torch,

I can't believe my eyes!

The gas turns on, the flame is lit,

And I begin my run,

Cheered on by endless crowds of people,

It was really lots of fun,

I passed it on, I did my job,

The flame reached London's games,

And each of us torch bearers,

Have a memory for the rest of days.

Summer Fun

Lying on a rug on a pebbly beach,

With the sea lapping up to the shore,

The ice cold treats from the ice cream shack,

Leaving us all wanting more.

The freezing cold sea, and jumping the waves,

Watching ships go off to other lands,

Collecting shells and building castles,

And leaving our imprints in the sand.

Sandy sandwiches, and lunch on the beach,

Sitting in the shade from the sun,

Once summer is here, we have no fear,

For we can always have some fun.

Oceans

On our world there are great oceans,

Coloured like crystal sapphires,

Expanding over most of the whole wide world,

An empire of vast enormity,

Never stopping, the oceans keep swimming,

Sloshing up the beach towards me.

Changing Tides

The sea comes up around my feet,

It's freezing cold on my feet,

The salty spray won't put me off,

I think I'll go for a swim.

The currents change directions,

As quick as we react,

And many parts of the changing tides,

Have on maps yet been tracked.

The crystal blue and the salty cold,

The beaches crowning glory,

It is the very heart and soul,

Of every summer story.

School Time

School time starts, you have a moan,

But you get on, you mustn't groan,

You mess around, you might work hard,

To get the grades on the piece of card,

But when school's well and truly gone,

You will know it paid off, if you didn't go wrong.

Sun, Sea, You and Me

Go down to the beach on a sunny day,

You won't be surprised by what you see,

Hundreds of people setting up,

Sun, sea, you and me,

Go for a paddle in the ocean blue,

Build a sandcastle fit for two,

The beach is where we all will be,

Sun, sea, you and me,

The end draws near, the sun dips low,

The tide draws up across the beach,

The day was fun, but we must go,

Sun, sea, you and me.

The Ticking Clock

Tick - tock, tick – tock,

The hands rotate on the spinning clock,

The clock goes back and time jumps round,

There's interference on the ground,

The glitch shuts off, and there's no time,

The clock resets, and everything's fine.

Gods and Monsters

Gods

Zeus

The king of the gods who rules the skies,

And governs all with an iron fist,

Whose lightning bolt is mighty feared,

That strikes from in the ominous mist.

Poseidon

The overlord of all the seas,

Whose trident symbol is well known,

Commanding waves of majestic height,

He makes the hulls of all ships groan.

Hades

Ruthless ruler of the deep dark depths,

The underworld is his domain,

He feeds upon our human fear,

Until he tries to rise again.

Athena

Wisdom is her mighty gift,

Bestowed upon a lucky few,

The strategist and cunning god,

Her wisdom is bestowed on you?

Aphrodite

Lady of love, and queen of hearts,

Our heartstrings her harps cords,

She used her love to bring us all,

Together with the lords.

Hermes

The lonely mailman of the gods,

The walks for all his days,

Upon the roads of gods and men,

This god has lost his ways.

Demigod

Half a god, and half a man,

With powers greater than the gods,

They can conquer many things,

Despite the low, enduring odds.

Monsters

Medusa

A tangle of snakes for serpentine hair,

And eyes who turn men to stone,

An enemy whose evil name,

Can leave a leader on his own.

Minotaur

A mighty beast of vile sight,

Its horns and hooves can strike a blow,

Believed to have been born on Crete,

To kill this creature, no one knows.

Siren

They lay upon the deadly rocks,

And lure our sailors to their doom,

By burning sun the look like girls,

But not by the revealing moon.

Centaur

Half a horse and half a man,

A mighty creature of mythical breed,

Can wield a sword or fire a bow,

A valiant and noble steed.

Hydra

A creature made of fear and dread,

It guards a fearsome open space,

For every head that you remove,

Two more will grow back in its place.

Cyclops

A giant man with just one eye,

Who wields a massive wooden bat,

To bring one down, a mighty man,

Will need to move quickly, like a cat.

Chimera

Part of serpent, lion and goat,

This beast is such a fearsome sight,

It has three heads with evil glares,

That stop all who gaze with fright.

Beyond the Woods

Out beyond the deep dark woods,

I do not know what you will see,

But there are many rumours,

Some of which were told to me.

The trees of ancient blackened wood,

With faces that do stare,

They guard the forest with their roots,

And all who enter there.

Past the forest and over the bridge,

You will find a river wide,

Many folks have tried to cross,

And all but one have drowned inside,

Should you cross the river, then

you'll see the mighty city high,

Where any item can be found,

And ships with balloons do fly,

The islands are chained together,

And float amongst the sky.

That is what lies beyond the deep dark woods.

Does Cupid Know?

Does cupid know that he has pierced my heart?

With arrows from his endless bow of love,

His love and intervention played a part,

In freeing the purest of my souls doves,

His love embrace did guide me all the way,

And lead me to my only one true love,

It's here with her that I will always stay,

And pace a ring upon her finger's glove,

Our love shall blossom, like the flowers bloom,

A hurricane could not tear us apart,

We'll be together unless love is doomed,

And that will cease the beating of my heart,

For everything as pure as love's true grace,

When love is gone, nothing can take its place.

The Armistice

The bell does sound and strike a chord

in every soldiers heart,

It marks the end of a brutal war,

Where many of us played our part.

The mindless deaths and gruesome scenes,

Will haunt us all our days,

In the darkest depths of our souls that can't

be pierced by bright sun rays,

This day does mark the start of peace,

And leaving Flanders fields behind,

For any survivor of a war,

Would not want to have remind,

He sacrifice the dead did make,

Who became one with the ground,

So on eleven a.m. forever more,

On this day we do not make a sound.

The Beginning is the End

As the beginning approaches,

The ending begins,

The change of an era,

And out with the in's,

The start is the finish,

The same thing in sight,

From the bright line of sunshine,

Comes the deep dark of night,

The rise and the falling,

As time walks on by,

The beginning is the final end,

We're born. We live. We die.

Money's Kiss

We own so very many things,

Most of which we rarely use,

So when it comes for us to decide,

We're spoilt when we have to choose,

In an age of ignorance and bliss,

Fate has lent us money's kiss.

Devil's Roots

You must not trust a single soul,

No matter where they stand,

For who knows where their devil's roots

have spread throughout the land.

They'll poison minds with doubt and fear,

Destroy all hearts good will,

Until their grip around our kingdom

keeps all people still.

Don't believe a thing you see,

You don't know if it's true,

For if it is, then run in fear,

The devil comes for you.

Deny your brain a single shred,

Of proof it sees or hears,

Or else the deaths of ones loved most,

Will draw from you your tears.

Playing With Heartstrings

I only met you just the once,

But that was all it took,

I fell head over heels for you,

Like a fish caught on a hook.

Your eyes were pools of emerald green,

Your hair shone bright as fire,

You wore your heart upon your sleeve,

And were my heart's desire,

The briefest chance we had to talk,

Your true colours shone through,

And with every beat of my heart,

I fell more in love with you.

You were the first love that I knew

was true inside my heart,

And from this my love only grew,

And you did play a part,

You occupied my thoughts,

Your beauty had ensnared me,

In your love trap I was caught.

But, then, unintentionally,

You found my secret true,

You told me how you really felt,

And my face turned downcast blue.

You took my heart with all its joy,

Accidentally of course,

And mad my love die out,

With an unnatural crushing force,

My life depressed and curled away,

In a recess of my mind,

And left me with my pool of tears,

All hope left behind.

I know it was an accident,

And that I can forgive,

But whenever I do think of you,

My heartstrings harp does play the blues.

Bubbles

Billowing in the endless wind,

Unknowing in their destination,

Brushing past the azure sky,

Blown into nothingness,

Lowering onto a surface to stick,

Endlessly they sit,

Suddenly they pop.

From Dawn to Dusk

From dawn to dusk,

I shall love you,

I'll prove it too,

From dawn to dusk.

From night till day,

By sour side I'll stay,

Not led astray,

From night till day.

From morning till evening,

My passion stays strong,

You're my love song,

From morning till evening.

From birth to death,

I love you still,

And always will,

From birth to death.

The Prize Giving

The sun dips low and we take our seats,

Only the spotlights guide our way,

We're dressed in our best, all eyes on the stage,

For today is prize giving day!

The music begins, our head teacher stands tall,

To deliver a powerful speech,

Then up stand the well renowned captains team,

And a kind word is said from each,

The performances start and we watch with awe,

As the events of the night do unfold,

Then slowly, one by one, each year

is beckoned and quietly told,

Come stand in line, your time has come

to collect your well-earned prize,

When you stand on stage, shake sir's hand with your right,

And try not to realise,

That a whole theatre of adults and students

are watching. Now up you go!

They nudge us forwards,

Up onto the stage,

It's time to put on a show!

The claps ring around, and the people do stand,

As we all take our temporary place,

We receive our reward for all our hard work,

And return to our seats with a smile on our face.

The curtains have closed, and the night has now ended,

The band closes the night with a cheer,

Both students and staff now both have a laugh,

We'll see you at prize giving next year!

One More Story

The night grows dark, and I lay down,

Upon my cosy bed,

My mother pulls my blanket up,

And kisses my forehead.

'When you wake up there will be snow,

And Santa will have been,

He'll eat the cookies that you have left out,

And leave presents under the tree'

She goes to turn out the light,

I call her back once more,

'Tell me another story' I say,

'Just one more, for sure'.

She sits back down, and begins her tale,

Of babies born in stables,

Of Santa's stuck in chimneys,

And mince pies left on tables,

She speaks of rings and partridges,

Within an old pear tree,

And flying reindeer with tiny elves,

Who are always watching me,

I close my eyes and fall asleep,

And dream of Christmas cheer,

I'm blessed by the light of the Christmas star,

For one day every year.

The Coming and Going of Christmas

The festive season draws so near,

The excitement builds inside,

The holidays are coming.

Advent calendars reappear,

Shops stock up on decorations,

The shopping madness starts.

School term ends, and kids go free,

The present pile builds up,

We stock food in large piles.

My shopping done, we wrap the gifts,

We put up the lights and the tree,

Christmas cheer is building.

Stockings full, and hyper kids,

The Christmas cheer explodes,

Christmas day is here.

The family gather in celebration,

We each hand out our gifts,

The fire of love and warmth burns bright.

The end comes close, the thirty first,

The wine comes out once more,

The next year's on its way.

All that's left is memories,

The tree is packed away,

Christmas is over, it's a new year.

Techno Trap

Nowadays society

Relies on pure invention,

To develop all our livelihoods

They say with good intention,

But technology is rising up,

As far as I can see,

It's taking over all our lives,

And not just you or me,

The techno trap is surely set,

The bait to lure us in,

They'll catch us in a metal cage,

And then from in the din,

It rises up and takes our place,

A surrogate of sorts,

With simply no emotion,

A uniformity of thoughts,

The trap is set, our time will come

And they will catch us all,

And with the rise of the machine,

Humanity will fall.

Alien (Where is everyone?)

The universe is mighty vast,

There's no way we're all alone,

They're out there, all across the stars,

On Jupiter, Saturn and even mars,

If the universe has really grown.

And grown so very fast,

Then where is everybody at?

When we look back into the past,

We light see aliens evolve,

They might see us as cavemen still,

Every time our earth revolves,

We might find them at last,

But where is everybody at?

Our livelihoods do move too fast,

To find them in one life,

They're out there, we just need to look,

Beyond our simple science book,

In amongst chaotic strive,

The universe is mighty vast.

That's where everybody's at.

Put Title Here

What is this object I have found?

It has no name and makes no sound.

What is this food that I shall eat?

It looks like fruit, but tastes like meat.

What is this fabric I can feel?

It looks like silk, but weighs like steel.

What is that object I can see?

I cannot tell what it could be.

What is the aroma I can smell?

Its odour makes me feel unwell.

What is this thing I cannot say?

Description seems to slip away.

What is this puzzle I can't solve?

The answer helped my mind evolve.

What is that thing I see inside?

Its name, from me is trying to hide.

What is this thing I'm thinking of?

Is it food, money, sleep or love?

Do any of these exist at all?

Put title here, and await my call.

The Blitz

We cower below,

While they fly overhead,

Whilst some of us live,

Many are dead,

The shelters are packed,

And not very nice,

But to stay alive,

It is but a small price,

For Adolf is after us,

Every single one,

And he will not stop,

Until his deeds are all done.

A Poets Destiny

It was as if a light bulb

just appeared above my head,

Before, the thought

had never crossed my mind,

But now I'm absolutely sure,

Of what I want to do,

Even though the latter

is to hide.

Locked away behind the bars,

My talent held behind,

Considered not quite right for modern times,

With nothing but the words I write

upon this scrap of paper,

I have nothing to testify but my rhymes.

Childhood Splendour

When I'm alone with my own mind,

I never know what I will find,

A long forgotten memory,

A person that I used to be,

My loves, hates, pride and joy,

Of once being a little boy,

Those days are gone, and I am old,

Forced to mature, by society's cold

unnerving gaze on all of the young,

Trapping their minds and wiping out fun,

For a child is always best to hide,

In the creativity of their mind.

Lionheart

A drop of sweat runs down my brow,

My men are here, the time is now,

We set up camp all through the night,

We hear the dark crusaders might,

My men are strong and show no fear,

Not even God can help us here,

Where these dark crusaders dwell,

We've passed into the mouth of hell,

The dawn draws close, and brings a chill,

The area is very still,

The fog draws in, obscures all sight,

Most likely we'll be dead tonight,

We mount our steeds, and start our ride,

With fear and patriotic pride,

We draw up close, their castle looms,

An omen of impending doom,

With my crown on my head, and my sword by my side,

As the lionhearted king I ride,

With all my men fighting back to back,

I call out the signal, and we begin our attack.

The Crusaders

The chorus clanged and clipped and caught,

Against the Lionheart we fought,

Our fortress made of strong hard stone,

We easily can hold our own,

Our archers pick them one by one,

And take them out in the morning sun,

The battle rages down below,

The fire casts an unearthly glow,

Our soldiers cut and swipe and slash,

And with their shields they bump and bash,

The bumbling Brits just blunder on,

We chase them down till they are gone,

The king rides in on noble steed,

And cuts our Frenchmen down with greed,

We double up and reappear,

We now attack them from the rear,

Our archers blot the sky with grey,

They cast their arrows in the fray,

We watch it go straight through his heart,

And thus the lion did depart.

No Escape

I'm trapped.

You cast your lines in dark waters,

Within your net I am caught,

Where you go I must follow,

My frantic heart is true distraught,

There's no escape for me.

I'm stuck.

Your snare pulled down the angels,

And dragged them into hell,

I cannot help but follow

the clang of a funeral bell,

There's no escape for me.

I'm caught.

My soul, you have encased it,

In a seal of iron lead,

As a phantom I do follow,

Your love was truly dead,

There's no escape for me.

I'm doomed.

The final gong has sounded,

The battle took all light away,

In blood soaked footsteps I shall follow,

Plunged into the darkest day,

There's no escape for me.

Think On Your Sins

Think on your sins,

And what you have done,

Think of your morals,

Have you really won?

Think of your conscience,

The weight you now bear,

The guilty shameful secret,

That you cannot, dare not share,

Think of your wrongs,

And who they will harm,

People aren't cattle,

For the slaughter on a farm,

Think of the problems your actions have caused,

Your brain cells have failed you,

Or else you'd have paused,

Think on your sins,

The debt must be paid,

The evil you shaped,

And the hell that you've made.

Nursery Nonsense – Part I

To lose a tail was a mighty price,

That was paid by the three blind mice,

It could be worse, because instead

they could have lost their little heads

The farmer's wife went completely mad,

And things indeed went rather bad,

Those stupid three blind mice.

Humpty dumpty was not cool,

In fact he was a great big fool,

To sit on a wall so very high,

Of course he surely was going to die,

The king's horses and men really did not care,

They had scrambled egg for breakfast there,

Humpty dumpty the dimwit.

Nursery Nonsense – Part II

I'll lock away my treacle and rice,

That weasel is not very nice,

He pops in here at any time,

And steals our stuff, it's like a crime!

That's the way my money goes,

He still comes back, it clearly shows,

I'll pop that bloody weasel.

Sheep can't talk they only go baa,

This one's wool is black as tar,

Three bags full is quite a lot,

From just one sheep? I think not,

It doesn't even get a say,

If it wanted to keep its wool that day,

The master the dame and the little boy down the lane!

Jack should have not gone up the hill,

With a little girl called 'lovely' Jill,

That devious and plotting witch,

Pushed him down the massive ditch,

She took the pail right back down,

And left Jack with a broken crown,

Silly Jack came crying back.

Bring Home the Boys

Bring home the boys, yes bring them all home!

A warzone is no place to be,

The horrors those men must see,

Trapped in a war, but long to be free.

Let them all leave, yes let them all leave!

Send them back to their loved ones dear,

Away from the war that's dull and drear,

Where safe in their arms there is nothing to fear.

Keep them all safe, just keep them all safe!

Out of the Taliban's way,

Every night and day,

Hear the words of the loved ones who pray.

Pull them all out, yes pull them all out!

Bring home our brave, bold boys,

Ignite cheer and glorious joy,

Just bring home, bring home the boys.

Pancakes

We crack the eggs and add the flour,

We give the concoction a mix,

Heat up a pan on the oven so warm,

And add oil so the mixture won't stick,

Pour in the mix, fry slowly in time,

Flip when you're halfway through,

Flip once more, don't drop of the floor,

'Grubs up' here's a pancake for you!

Love Games

The 14th is the starting line,

If the annual love games,

Where men compete across the world,

To win the hearts of dames,

With cards and gifts and chocolate,

To woo their appetites,

And gain access to their land of love,

To love them in their life,

Why put yourself through all the pain,

When you often have simply nothing to gain?

Ballad for a Deserving Mum

The kindest spirit you will know,

The nicest person you will meet,

Her loving nature put on show,

Matriarch of the family fleet,

She comes for us like natures call,

Helps us grow, to be the best,

She picks us up when we do fall,

Better than any and all the rest,

Ballad of the brave and true.

Mum, this poem is for you.

Hard at work both day and night,

Without her we would all be lost,

Her response is always right,

Always worth it, whatever the cost,

Her fondness a protective screen,

A smokescreen or a shroud,

We won't be hurt, we are a team,

She always makes us proud,

Golden like the rising sun,

We love you, dear deserving mum.

Tale of the Treasure Temple

It is said ten thousand years ago,

An ancient city ruled the land,

Ruled by king, and ruled by queen,

The emperors stood hand in hand,

Their influence spread far and wide,

They ruled the land, the sea, the sky,

Worshipping their ancient gods,

The citadel was placed up high,

Rich they were, with jewels and gold,

Beyond our wildest dreams,

So rich in fact, that everyone

would bathe in golden streams,

Of crowns and coins, of jewels and gold,

They prized one thing above it all,

The colour of pure amethyst,

Their eternal crystal ball,

They looked to it for answers true,

A gift of the gods they would say,

The dials at its base would turn,

It would lead them every day,

But then one day it did predict,

A villain close at hand,

An enemy so powerful,

It would destroy all their land,

Whilst war ensued, they gathered up,

All their precious worth,

And hid them in the citadel,

In hope of safety and rebirth,

The battle raged, the crystal showed,

Their imminent demise,

The people of the empire watched,

They could not believe their eyes,

The chamber locked, the treasure kept,

Behind lock and chain and key,

The final order was sent out,

The people told to flee,

The king and queen now dead and gone,

The city pulled down to the ground,

The temple is still hidden though,

The treasures waiting to be found,

The sighs of the dead don't make a sound,

Yet still the tale of the treasure temple,

Echoes through the valley's rift.

Perfection in Disguise

The moon illuminates the sky,

An iridescent violet hue,

Everything I see this night,

Does only make me think of you.

The sapphire blue of the rippling waves,

Reflects to me your eyes,

It seems like nature is your mask,

Perfection in disguise.

The ochre brown of sturdy oaks,

Your hair flows long and smooth,

We both stand tall like sturdy trees,

Together we planted our roots.

The scent of roses pierce the air,

A smell divine and true,

Your sweetness, I see everywhere,

Your likeness pouring through.

Within the stars I see your face,

Shining up above,

You're always looking out for me,

Pure, like a gleaming dove.

The softness of the silent grass,

Caresses, cold, just like your skin,

The smoothest touch so sensual,

You stir my soul within.

The night bird song does fill my ears,

As enchanting as your voice,

It lures me in, just like you did,

As if I had a choice!

My love, I see you everywhere,

The goodness of your heart

shines through and makes all nature sing,

Glowing, pulsing in the dark.

Easter Evolution

It was nigh two thousand years ago,

When Easter did begin,

Spring, rebirth and giving,

Did strip away our sin,

Time evolved, tradition stayed,

And now we celebrate,

By giving people boiled eggs

we paint and decorate,

A sign of friendship and new starts,

Like new born baby chicks,

A time of smiles and of laughs,

And chocolate hunting tricks,

The celebrations grew and grew,

And markets got involved,

With the new industrial tweak,

Again, Easter evolved,

It became a time for boys and girls,

With chocolate eggs galore,

Milk, white, dark, sweet, creamy,

We always wanted more,

Wrapped in foil like golden gifts,

Treasures given to kings,

Easter eggs both big and small,

Do make a chocoholic sing,

Such a wide variety,

Of every flavour shape and size,

They look so good, and taste so swell,

You won't believe your eyes,

If, two thousand years ago,

Easter did not start,

It would not have won a very special place,

In every child's heart.

Through the Static

Static through the speaker grill,

Not a sound is heard,

A song would be preferred,

It gives me quite a chill.

White noise fills the place,

The universe rolls silently by,

While our instruments watch the sky,

That vacuum of empty space.

We stare back in time,

The signals sent from long ago,

Received on earth, we're just too slow,

Its beauty so sublime.

As nature takes its course,

Worlds collide –

Stars have died,

With deadly power, cosmic force.

A noise comes through the speaker grill,

We don't know what to do,

We didn't think it through,

The room goes deadly still,

First contact, not a drill.

Calling IQ

Why not give it another go?

If you didn't figure out my code,

Well done I say, bravo!

You put your IQ to the test,

Is this all just a dream?

Do aliens exist at all?

What lies in-between?

If life is death and death is life,

Considering you've made it this far.

Let's just see how good you are,

,front to back line this put I'll

I can make it harder if you want,

Will you solve it at all?

The code is hidden in such plain sight,

The answer to life's true call?

Six times sever is… forty two,

I hope you've got some time.

Let's put your IQ to the test,

Can you solve this rhyme?

How clever do you think you are?

Winter Receding

Winter's ending brings the spring,

Hardness, natures softening

of cold clod earth

and misty breeze that rattles through the trees.

Further down, now far below,

The flowers do begin to grow,

The reign of winter does recede,

Into showers, fragmented, vapour

trails in the sky of a once cold land,

The golden tendrils whisper past,

Regenerating lifeless trees,

Long lost time regathered thus,

The leaves now turn a shade of green,

And brighten the world for us.

Lakes upon the bluest blue,

Like sapphires hanging in the sky

do play home to new found birds,

And lambs will frolic in the fields

as nature passes by.

The golden light that does restore,

Brings life and hope forever more.

Words Hurt

You hear it.

Whispers.

Dancing in the night around your soul.

Intertwined, with lace and black promises,

Broken.

I stand

Alone.

Voices through a wall,

Tendrils of vowels and consonants

drag me back,

lips, vicious. Like a beast.

Words. Hurt.

Light

Like gossamer, weightless,

Illuminates the dust within the sunbeams,

Giving warmth, life to old bones,

Helping raise the cold from the ground,

Tendrils of gold, whispers on the wind.

The City of the Dark

As darkness fell, the blackness rolled in,

The days turned sour; the peace broken.

The master has now come to collect his debts,

No more, no less.

We, like children, cower in our cradles,

With feeble prayer and sobs of pure fear,

Sweat runs down our brows like tears of salt,

The collector draws near.

Drops fall out of the sky.

Not rain, no

The vilest blackest drops of evil,

Burning a path from hell to the deliverer,

They eat their way

Through stone and steel,

Devil's breath rising from their paths,

Screams pierce the dark, thick air,

As the deliverer descends.

Fires rage and pen us in,

Houses smoke, and people choke,

Super-heated, gushing claws,

Reaching for the living,

As he pulls them back away,

Materialising through the hellish scenes,

The four horsemen have come to play,

For Death, has come today.

The Light in the Darkness

As darkness fell across the land,

Light did shine on through,

Hope amongst the devil's rage,

But only for a few.

The fires drowned, the purged, they cleansed

the city of its sin,

Light surrounded the virtuous ones within,

Encasing them in godly light,

Out of reach of him.

The deliver slashed, and took their souls,

While those in light flew high above,

Their virtue shone bright,

Delivered unto caring arms,

Outside the singing golden gates,

Where angels do abide.

The glowing warmth of goodly light,

Did warm their precious hearts,

As new hell rages down below,

The good watch on as now they know,

They were spared the horsemen's hooves.

Sin outweighs virtue and weighs you down,

Into the dark, where there is no sound,

The earth is cleansed, like Noah's ark,

With those of good to start again,

He chose them to survive the storm,

For them, true death will never come.

Taking the Throne

As I sit and stare,

My mind wanders

to world unknown and scenes unshown,

To distant lands where I alone

do sit upon the throne.

Consciousness is like a big dream,

So easy to dismiss,

Yet ever so poignant.

Those distant lands are always mine,

Wherever I shall go,

For in my own subconscious,

I always take the throne.

The Stone Eye

Endlessly it glares,

Like a phantom of the plains,

Seeing all, observing nothing,

A void of creation.

Transfixed, it stays,

Caught in a perpetual glow,

Translucent, yet blind,

It fumbles into nothingness.

Lidless and lifeless,

Lost in the wilderness,

Consumed by fecund, fetid decay,

Flesh, no more.

The blackness hides

twisted figures and hooded corpses,

All the same, all lost

while searching for purpose.

Lifeless. Like a gorgon's eye

It peers into you,

Turning the soul to stone.

We Are the Dead

We are the dead.

Nought can save

the men who died in Flanders fields,

And lie beyond the grave.

We are dust.

Memories only,

Fading. Forgotten.

We are the lost.

The ghosts, the damned,

Buried in the mud and sand.

Poppies mark our passing ways,

Remembrance, for the end of days.

Clock

Counting forwards, backwards, stop.

Longingly pulling at reality,

Only important when there's not enough,

Cleverly deceptive,

Key to the future.

Crowd

My identity is lost,

I am no longer myself,

Within this crowd I am just a figure,

A statistical value

of no importance.

We act like this to hide,

In a crowd we are safe – at least

until we find our identity.

Once we know who we are,

We are separate from society,

Exposed. They can see us,

We can run, but there is

no safety in numbers,

Identity is life's great struggle,

And it's achievement

is singling you out.

Then they find you,

Then they take you.

My identity is lost, I'm never found,

They'll never find me.

Have Your Say

I have found my way with words,

But this might not suit you,

So dig down deep inside yourself,

And you'll find your way too.

Be it pictures, word or dance,

Stick strong, and be true,

Show us all just how you feel,

Your expression will come through,

It will change your life in every way,

So stand up, speak out, and have your say.

By the Light of the Moon

An iridescent, beauteous glow,

New features of us that we see,

The pebble tossed into the lake,

The cooling, moonlit breeze.

Ripples spread on surface,

A distorted, reflective sheen,

Thick darkness, diluted by pure white light,

An aura of a dream.

Aurora pulse above our heads,

The night alive with dancing flames,

But when they die, and dark resumes,

Nothing looks the same.

I hold your hand, you hold my heart,

In this moonlit, mirrored space,

And out on wild Elysian fields,

Two minds as one do race.

The ripples move, our image merged,

Two souls combined as one,

Pulsing, glowing bold as brass,

The will of hearts is done.

In distant light we move as one,

A single being, effortless

we glide across the glades,

Moonlights law is undeceiving.

The silent glow begins to waver,

Time pushes blood-light into view,

For we must part, our heart of hearts,

Too soon, I lose sight of you.

For only can we be lovers,

By the light of the moon.

Brimstone Inferno

Deep, deep down, within your mind,

In manacles and chains you'll find,

An evil darker side to you,

In your subconscious it grew,

It fed on fear and angst and hate,

Its mission: to eradicate

your hopes and dreams, your pride and joy,

To play with you just like a toy,

For countless years it hid away,

Now it wants to come and play,

The vile snake constricts around,

Pummels who you were to the ground,

Instead, standing in your place,

Is a villainous and vile race,

Born in brimstone, hate and fire,

It serves your ID, your deep desire,

The battle of the mind is tough,

Do you even think you're strong enough?

Drowned in its inferno ways,

Lost you are, for all your days.

The Human Condition

The human condition is quite complex,

It can be concave or convex,

Identity is key for us,

When grappling the tower of society,

The ladder so high, few reach the peak.

We judge on personality,

Colour, race and individuality,

If as a group we do not fit,

We're cut off because of it.

Human nature can be cruel,

And treat our species like a fool,

But then, there's kindness, hope and love,

That lift society high up,

Above the prejudice and hate,

We can be kind and caring souls,

We can be cruel villainous wrecks,

The human condition dictates our moves,

Like pieces in a game of chess,

It's not too hard to understand,

We all get dealt a different hand.

My Identity

I float, lifeless on the breeze,

Nature dictates my journey's course,

Civilisation passes by,

I am unaffected – unchanged

by bombardments of media and press,

Constant tells to change my ways,

I float by, they cannot reach.

The wind pulls me to the floor,

With a jolt, I open my eyes,

I know who I am, my identity.

I am awake.

Black Hole

The vortex swirls,

The wind whirls,

All is sucked inside,

Stars crushed,

Time rushed,

A star that's gone and died.

All dead,

Above our heads,

There's nowhere safe to hide.

Superhero

The ending is nigh,

My powers overwhelmed him,

I am in control,

The city does burn.

His evil scheme was foiled,

I, am the hero.

For justice I fight,

Taking down villains like him,

And saving the world.

The Blank Page

I sit and stare...   the page is blank.

Waiting for my artist's hand,

I CAN DO AS I WILL, MAKE WHAT I WANT,

The page is **mine.**

I can pour out every single thought,

AND splash it on the page,

The tools sit calmly and await my call,

I reach my hand, and take the pen.

Think spreads on the paper.

MY *ideas* bloom.

Forever young

(Co-written with Elysia Salmon)

The drop that drinks a thousand years,

A breath for rugged lungs,

To cleanse the withered face and soul,

To make the broken body whole,

Life cascading down the drain

replenished.

The tower of Bimini's gold,

A land once lost, forever old,

A liquid cloak from claws of death,

Forever young, a curse of life,

Prettied by legend and foolish men,

Who dream of being young again.

The tongue that speaks a thousand lies,

Cocooned in holy waters,

Drowning out the song of sun,

When life meets death they merge as one,

A never ending prison cell,

Trapped, inside a wishing well,

Drowned, while nothing looks the same,

While others sleep inside their grave, I am forever young.

Army in red

(Co-written with Elysia Salmon)

Devoid of life they stand,

Ad army seven thousand strong,

Upholding the emperor's land,

One whose reign is now long gone.

Immortalised through sand and stone,

Empty shells of life once lost,

An army of neither blood nor bone,

On history they have been embossed.

Honour, grace and majesty,

Colossal graves beneath archaic earth,

Killer Qin-Shi's cavalry,

Priceless in their ancient worth.

While these warriors slumber on,

Dynasties have passed them by,

Awaiting the sound of an emperor's gong,

Sleepless, the army in red do lie.

Unblemished they have hidden for years,

Like pieces in a game of chess,

No love, no hate, no pride, no fears,

The red will rise, no more, no less.

Siren song

Stranded on my rock,

I call across the water,

Calling out to man,

Drawing their ships towards me,

My body glistens,

My aquatic nature clear,

I draw them closer,

Foolish men come for a kiss,

I devour them.

H2O

Endlessly I ripple,

Gliding across the surface like a sunbeam,

Trickling a trail across the earth.

Cool on skin, home to life,

I glint and gleam like sapphires,

Lapping shores of distant lands,

Quenching parched throats,

I hide the deepest secrets,

I am the H_2O.

Animal collection

Cat

Cute and furry feline friend,

Curling on the sofa,

Soft purring while you sleep,

Companion throughout.

Cow

Splodges of black and white,

Dotted across the fields,

Making milk and methane,

A grass loving giant.

Koala

Eating eucalyptus leaves,

As cute and cuddly as can be,

A legacy down under,

Clinging to the trees.

Giraffe

Giant necks and tiny heads,

Reaching for the tallest trees,

Roaming the savannah plains,

One of a zoo's must see's.

Scorpion

A fearsome desert survivalist,

One sting can fell a man,

Stalking the sand in the blistering heat,

This cunning creature hatches a plan.

Fish

Big and small they grace the seas,

A wide range of varieties,

Splashes of colour in the ocean blue,

A shoal of aquatic societies.

Platypus

Semi-aquatic unusual thing,

With a tail and a bill,

Both land and water skilled,

And egg laying mammal.

Magpie

Shooting sky rocket,

Snatching the shiny,

Building up a treasure nest,

Their plunder is never tiny.

Zebra

Black and white, or white and black?

Bounds across the open plains,

A hungry lion's favourite snack,

The speedy stripes win their games.

The Earthworm

The silent friend to solid earth,

Cold clod turned to fertile land,

Recycling, it rejuvenates,

So tiny within the grand

scheme of things, so small,

And yet so pivotal.

The farmer's closest ally,

To grow his crops and make his wage,

Day by day, no change with age,

At threat in dawn,

By shadowed wings,

Devouring the little things,

So pink and soft, so squirmy,

The sound of rain driving them upwards.

Up, up to the surface,

Feeling the light on their skin,

Then down, deep below the earth,

Down they go, and further still,

The farmer's songs the earthworms sing.

The Wire Man

My edges sharp and cold to touch,

Fragile and flexible I stand,

Weakened by the ways of man,

Fibres breaking strand by strand,

My structure buckles,

Then it breaks,

The world of wire men shakes,

Flexible, we fold and change,

Our structure never stays the same,

So real, and yet invisible.

The Gingerbread Man

The steam cools off,

The figure shows,

Gingerbread in rows and rows,

Gumdrop buttons adorn their chest,

Choc-chip eyes that look their best,

Their icing hair and little shoes,

To make the little figures real,

And finally, a cheeky smile,

To make the men all taste worthwhile.

A Philosophy on Fun

I read up on the so called laugh mechanics,

The lectures of the theory of fun,

Philosophies and geographies,

It all sounds like monotonies,

A joke-a-holic's vine is surely spun.

The happiness patrol is but a fiction,

A way to keep your mind at rest and ease,

The end is just the starting line,

The happy hour's only fine,

When you've had too much to drink and fall asleep.

I don't agree with joyous celebration,

A waste of time when fun is but a myth,

But laughter is a remedy,

To cure the sad, and steadily,

Without our smiles, our lives grow dull and stiff.

A concept, fun is difficult to grasp at,

A distant thought, a memory of life,

When put under the microscope,

What you see does give you hope,

Philosophies on fun are rather nice.

Blood Rose

Dark crimson,

Like pure blood drawn from raw lips,

Concealing a daggered gaze,

Dripping like candle wax to the cold floor.

Silk.

Soft, yet so deadly,

Cloaking the staggered truth,

Fragile, like a vase,

Blood red petals, falling,

The failing glow splattered by dark light.

Stem by stem, colour fading,

Blood turning to cold hard pewter.

Dead and lifeless, drooping down,

Ended by grief and dark jaws,

Blackened by charcoal claws,

Drank by greedy pools.

Dark crimson,

Tears drained down the face,

The dead heart does disgrace.

Days Untold

I see your face within the crowd,

I know it's you for sure,

Smiling to myself, I think,

We've met like this before.

That night the first of many times,

We laughed and loved and shared,

Underneath the gods and stars,

No love could be compared.

Throughout the years our blossom grew,

As pure soul light we shone,

Our love spread like a wildfire,

The angels sang our song.

The time grew late, our days grew old,

The fire dwindled to an ember,

The days long gone, with angel song,

Are ones we will remember.

You held my hand and drew your breath,

The light grew dim and cold,

I kissed your cheek and love you still,

For all the days untold.

I see your face within the crowd,

I know this can't be true,

For you died not too long ago,

And my heart does lie with you.

Writers Block

I'm stuck.

I don't know what to write or say,

I've got the mind to make ends meet,

It could go either way.

I've drawn the strands,

I've changed my mind,

To write or not, to write or not?

The pen sits. My mind thinks,

The wall is nigh impossible,

I grab a thought, I start to climb,

I climb the blocking mountain high,

To reach the top I start to write,

I write a word. Sentence. Rhyme.

I'll overcome the wall this time,

I smash the wall, it tumbles down,

Another stands before me.

The Fallen Angel

You fight for all that's right and good,

A hero in a bitter war,

You battled gods and fiendish men,

But fell down at the devil's door,

You fought across the Satan pit,

Through sulphur clouds and the deadly dark,

The fiend's servants on your tail,

Evil pulsing like a spark.

Exiled from protective light,

Fallen from the golden track,

You fell into the devil's grasp,

Your soul is lost, you can't come back,

There was a time the light was home,

You served the kings and mighty gods,

Defender of the good and pure,

Fighting off evil against all odds,

But Adam and Eve broke down your door,

The snake coiled tight around your chest,

With no choice but to do his will,

You slew the gods and all the rest,

With Lucifer on every side,

Your wings were clipped, and you were thrown

out of the light, down into the darkness

to be forgotten.

Time passed, you grew,

Your power strengthened by blood and fear,

Until you rose and Beelzebub,

The name no mortal wants to hear,

You took your seat beside the throne,

Your devils danced around your head,

No conscience, soul, life or love,

Your innocence was lost and dead.

The darkness grew, you waged a war,

On the disciples of the light,

You tore apart the worldly bonds,

Turning brightest day to blackest night,

Your war raged on far overhead,

While humans cowered and prayed,

To be cloaked from your cleaver claws,

To be protected, to be saved.

They speak of your in legend,

The one who fell for the Devil's tricks,

A lesson learned, a promise made,

The story of a fallen angel.

Winter Wind

Winter wind whips through the trees,

A bitter frost that's blown for days,

The leafless branches swish and swash,

Dancing in a winded daze,

The path once soft now cold and hard,

The ice cracks on the ground,

The flowers crusted in a crystal glaze,

Nought but wind makes a sound,

The icy world surrounds my gaze,

A wondrous sight to behold,

The snow that falls upon my face,

Only a moment old,

The glistening white, the biting cold,

The whistle of the whispering winds,

Frozen Ice-land covers lakes,

The music of winter sings.

The white so pure and cold, so fierce,

Like snowfire, bright it shone,

Then break of day took all away,

This winter, two days gone.

Stolen Soul

Oh, whatever happened to your soul?

Where did the life, the love, the joy go,

From that girl I used to know?

Your mind is like an armoured suit,

Nothing can get past,

To warm your frozen blood,

And bring to life your stone cold heart.

You used to be so bright,

You would shine in every room,

Now you're hiding in the gloom.

You lost your smile, you lost your love,

He threw you like a doll,

Your china face has splintered,

Then he tore and burnt your soul,

You close your mind to others,

To protect yourself from harm,

No man will see your charm,

You hide your life away,

So you're not led astray,

No love, no light of day.

Dawn of the Dead

And now the end has come at last,

The final break of day,

Our foes still haul their heavy hammers,

We'll face them, come what may.

We are the strong, we are the brave,

The mighty men of home,

Defending our lady, her power, her hour,

Souls left free to roam.

We walk among the ravaged earth,

No land that looks like Eden,

Trapped like rats in an endless maze,

To die, we win our freedom.

The dead they turn inside their graves,

Of mud and mangled bone,

The long long lost, both British and Bosche,

Lost, left, alone.

The whistle sounds, we make our push,

The bombs, their awful sound,

Our souls now free, we take our leave,

To join those underground.

The Journalist

Once we were respected.

We who used to break the news,

Now we seem to make the news,

Our common cause rejected.

Now, I'm a liar,

A social pariah,

Tossed into the fire,

An untrusted man.

All those spycams and hackings,

They sully our name,

Take the walk of "shame",

It's YOU we are tracking.

Unnoticed, invisible, the fly on the wall,

Ready for anything, we're on the ball,

We aim to tread high, but we make the dark fall,

Into the jaws of social corruption.

We'll tell you the headlines, the stories, the "proof",

But honestly, we're no harbingers of truth,

We're not simpletons, but in the age of the youth,

The stories keep on spinning.

We jump at the chance to get you alone,

To probe the secrets inside your head,

And print the things you truly dread,

Like the cold west wind once blown.

Say what you like, we're ready to strike!
You call me a snoop? Oh no! Not at all!

I'm a journalist.

New Life

As one does end, another begins,

Re-birth, to step out of the light,

New life to wash away your sins,

Pure, clean and bright,

Walk this earth with joyous soul,

You move as one with all your kind,

Strong and smart, you reach your goal,

To leave the condemned and dead behind,

Brighten up the darkest place,

Saviour of the weary folk,

The halo's light upon your face,

To them your guidance is no joke,

Your light shines brightly everywhere,

Re birth is life, your joy to share.

Change

Time comes for all to change,

The old steps aside for the new,

The world seems so so strange,

Out of contact, out of range.

Has it come to this?

Where lives are lost,

Without a kiss,

Forgotten in the mist?

We don't all want to move on,

And experience something new,

The next chapter of our song,

Afraid that things will go wrong.

Change will come either way,

You have to adapt or lose out,

Only one can truly stay,

If not tomorrow, change is today.

We're never ready when it comes,

But we face it all in all,

Change propels us forwards,

It helps us fly and fall.

Change is inevitable.

Snowy Gold

The dead wind blows behind your back,

The fear before the fall,

The chance for glory and the pride of your nation,

You can win it all,

The ice wind whips across the plains,

Winter forest's silent sound,

Snowfall lights your footsteps as

they crunch across the frozen ground.

The claxon sounds, you spur yourself on,

Through sleet and fog and fear,

The whistling wind carries up from below,

The sound of distant cheer,

Roll the dice, take the risk,

Go for broke, flat out.

The nation standing side by side,

To cheer and scream and shout,

Cross the line, breathe relief,

You fought the claws of cold,

And like the songs and legends of old,

We claim the snowy gold.

Possessive Dread

Is this it? Has it come to this?

Where demon hounds roam the halls,

When Alcatraz would feel like home,

Caught, preserved inside a dome.

The mists of treachery descend,

And blur ones vision steadily,

Fooling the incompetent mind,

Death's too quick for your such kind,

Twisted souls ad mangled screams,

Echo through your stone cold heart,

The lightning rages with the storm,

Deep within, it takes its form.

Crashing waves wash out your mind,

Possession takes its hollow grip,

Devils hooves become your tread,

What once you were is buried and dead.

The voices speak inside your mind,

The boiling fire that burns beneath,

Lost and gone, you've drowned and died,

Sadistic traps snapped short your pride.

The demon hounds still roam the halls,

Pulsing, cursed and feral death,

Darkness rises, the lighthouse falls.

Light Therapy

Sheath your clouded thoughts,

And sit among the pillowed greens,

Rest your heart, your mind, your soul,

Wash out the midnight dreams.

Dampened hearts dry out in time,

Sunlight shines on darkened days,

Once broken and bent is shaped again,

The brightest buttercup rays.

Never contained by chains or bars,

Free minds roam in the sky,

Moonlight shines while sunlight finds,

Honest souls cannot die.

Lost in fog and quicksand thoughts,

Release your mind, let freedom reign,

Love blossoms sure as tulips grow,

Joyous life with little pain.

Brightened woods filled the mind,

Freedom of ways to choose,

Sunlight pierces the cleaned soul,

Free life can't be refused.

Concealing My Truth

Trapped inside a hollow skin,

Too scared to share my thoughts,

Afraid of rejection, abandonment,

And bullied mindless taunts.

I cannot speak my true self true,

For society deems it wrong,

I can't be unique, I was warned to conform,

Injustice sings its song.

I hide amongst the 'normal' man,

They do not care for those like me,

To conceal my true façade,

I wear a mask for all to see.

My loved ones dear may turn away,

They do not know for who I am,

And if they should, I fear they would,

Not love me like the babe raised from the pram.

I steal away in fear of hurt,

To myself and those I love,

For judgement day is too close to say,

I will get no peace, no white dove.

One day I'll tell my secret true,

Till then I hide myself from view.

Synaesthesia

Purple, yet your eyes see violet,

Gazing into the distance,

A reminder of purity.

Red, yet your lips taste crimson,

Pressing false kisses,

Drawing blood from every breath.

White, yet you feel cold as diamond,

Brittle to touch,

So delicate, so deadly.

Yellow, yet you sound like gold,

Rich and enchanting,

A treasured relic.

Black, yet you smell of darkness,

Drawn unto the night,

To abandon me.

You and I

I'll wait.

All day, all year,

I'll still be here,

Until you are ready to face it.

I'll stay.

You need me more than you know,

You just won't let it show,

I can save you.

I'll go.

You need to learn it tough,

Life is harsh and rough,

You need me.

I'm here.

I was never really gone,

As a guiding light I shone,

Come to me.

Stay near.

We can't afford to lose ourselves,

We're bound together now,

Forever, until beyond death,

I. Love. You.

The Wait

I feel my nerves inside me,

The worry, doubt and dread,

The fear that knots my stomach,

And makes me want to shout,

The hardest part is over,

And now the wait begins,

To see if I have passed the test,

To see if I get in,

My future is out of my hands,

My fate the choice of someone else, it seems

there's nothing I can do,

But wait and hope and dream,

I clear my mind of doubtful thoughts,

But they always crawl back in,

The agonising, slow-paced wait,

It's drawing my patience thin,

The day will come, and soon in fact,

Where I will hear my fate,

My future hinges on that moment,

But for now I simply wait.

An Unforeseen Engagement

To even think about it now,

My heart beats faster still,

To dream that I could be with you,

It gives me quite a thrill.

When I sit and talk with you,

I feel blissfully at peace,

The more I sit and gaze at you,

My feelings just won't cease.

To me you are a perfect soul,

You make me feel alive,

I hope to god you feel the same,

As one our love could thrive.

Your face encaptures perfectly,

A pure angelic grace,

A simple, vibrant presence,

Makes the room a brighter place.

To me you're an Adonis,

Perfection to my eyes.

To spend my days and years with you,

Is far greater than any prize.

You make my heartbeat skip with joy,

And dream during the day,

Of how we would spend our precious time,

Of what we'd do or say.

I think you do not notice,

That I have feelings for you,

So, one day, when I'm brave enough,

I'll tell you something new.

You sweep me straight off my feet,

You make my mind run wild,

It's unconventional and unforeseen,

But has been born of cupid's child.

I really don't know what to do,

But I think I've fallen in love with you.

The Kiss

At first, it was just innocent,

A date,

A chance to meet,

Yet it seemed that fate had other plans.

The coffee warmed our frozen thumbs,

We talked and smiled,

Something begun,

A blueprint being drawn into the sand.

The sun gone down we went to walk,

And sat atop the hill,

The peaceful sound and soft-glow lights,

I remember clear as crystal still.

You leaned in close,

Your eyes shone bright,

Our faces close as you dare,

Then your lips brushed mine,

And I had no other care.

My brain shut down.

I turned to sand,

You surprised me to my core,

That night, the first,

I could never forget,

I changed forever more.

Like fireworks inside my mind,

My pulse raced rocket high,

You sent me to utopia,

On cloud nine in the sky.

Sensations that I never thought,

Were possible to feel,

Through our nervous, awkward kiss,

Suddenly were real.

That kiss the first, but not the last,

My heart glowed like the sun,

I think it's only fair to say,

That night, something had begun.

Chapter One

It seems this chapter has an end,

I've filled to the brim my first page,

It's been a long and bumpy road,

But I have developed as I age,

The end of act one has come at last,

A rollercoaster ride,

So much has happened in this part,

I feel a sense of pride,

For I have grown into a man,

And changed in many ways,

I've held on to and followed my dreams,

I've seen the brightest days,

But there have been rocky bumps,

And difficult times too,

I've made it out the other side,

But still have work to do,

The stage is being set as I speak,

Act two is set to start,

There is no script, no lines or plan,

So I'll follow the instincts of my heart.

Chapter two begins…

To be continued…

Acknowledgements

There are several people I would like to thank for their support both with the book, and with helping me develop as a young writer. Firstly, the largest thank you I can make goes to my parents, for always having an unwavering belief in me, even when I didn't believe in myself. Without their support I doubt I would ever have had the confidence to be myself and follow my passions. Without the support of my mum and dad, I would not be who I am today, and this book would not exist. Secondly, thank you to my English teacher Peter Harris, for helping me to discover my talent, and providing me with the support and materials to pursue and develop my craft. I would also like to thank my friend, and fellow poet Elysia Salmon, with whom I wrote two of these poems; 'Forever young' and 'Army in red'. The many times we bounced ideas and inspiration off of each other, and acted as guinea pigs for each other's material seem to have paid off, so thank you for all the help and support.

Finally, a huge thank you goes to my friend and fellow author Melissa Holden, without whom this book would never have been published. Your knowhow and experience has helped me to achieve a lifelong dream, and so for that I will be forever grateful.

That's all for now, so I guess I'll see you on the other side in chapter two…

Printed in Great Britain
by Amazon.co.uk, Ltd.,
Marston Gate.

11657107R00145